Primary Maths for Scotland

2nd Level Maths

2A

Practice Workbook 1

© 2024 Leckie

001/01082024

10 9 8 7 6 5 4 3 2 1

ISBN 9780008680336

Published by
Leckie
An imprint of HarperCollins Publishers
Westerhill Road, Bishopbriggs, Glasgow, G64 2QT

T: 0844 576 8126 F: 0844 576 8131
leckiescotland@harpercollins.co.uk www.leckiescotland.co.uk

HarperCollins Publishers
Macken House, 39/40 Mayor Street Upper, Dublin 1, D01 C9W8, Ireland

Publisher: Fiona McGlade

Special thanks
Project editor: Peter Dennis
Layout: Jouve
Proofreader: Julianna Dunn

A CIP Catalogue record for this book is available from the British Library.

Acknowledgements
Images © Shutterstock.com

Printed in India by Multivista Global Pvt. Ltd.

Contents

Answers

Check your answers to this workbook online: https://collins.co.uk/pages/scottish-primary-maths

1.1 Rounding whole numbers to the nearest 10

1 Round these numbers to the nearest 10. You can use the number lines to help you.

a) 21 [ ]   b) 24 [ ]   c) 26 [ ]   d) 25 [ ]

```
20  21  22  23  24  25  26  27  28  29  30
```

e) 259 [ ]   f) 251 [ ]   g) 255 [ ]   h) 253 [ ]

```
250  251  252  253  254  255  256  257  258  259  260
```

i) 702 [ ]   j) 708 [ ]   k) 704 [ ]   l) 706 [ ]

```
700  701  702  703  704  705  706  707  708  709  710
```

m) 2749 [ ]   n) 2742 [ ]   o) 2744 [ ]   p) 2745 [ ]

```
2740  2741  2742  2743  2744  2745  2746  2747  2748  2749  2750
```

2 Which numbers can be rounded up or down to **310** when they are rounded to the nearest 10?

Write three possible answers in the boxes, then complete the number line to check.

[ ]   [ ]   [ ]

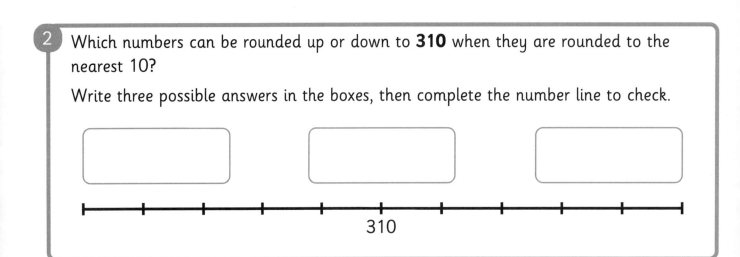

```
            310
```

3 Which numbers can be rounded up or down to **5790** when they are rounded to the nearest 10?

Write three possible answers in the boxes, then complete the number line to check.

5790

4 Which numbers can be rounded up or down to **5070** when they are rounded to the nearest 10?

Write three possible answers in the boxes, then complete the number line to check.

5070

5 Which numbers can be rounded up or down to **6800** when they are rounded to the nearest 10?

Write three possible answers in the boxes, then complete the number line to check.

6800

6 Which numbers can be rounded up or down to **7000** when they are rounded to the nearest 10?

Write three possible answers in the boxes, then complete the number line to check.

7000

7 Finlay has asked Nuria to mark his work. Write a ✔ beside the answers that are correct, and correct the ones that are wrong.

a) 31 rounded to the nearest 10 is **30**.

b) 55 rounded to the nearest 10 is **50**.

c) 456 rounded to the nearest 10 is **460**.

d) 505 rounded to the nearest 10 is **500**.

e) 7597 rounded to the nearest 10 is **7590**.

f) 8996 rounded to the nearest 10 is **8990**.

★ Challenge

1. Write five numbers that, when rounded to the nearest 10, would give **100**.

2. Use the clues to choose the correct number from the suggestions below. Circle your choice.

3853	8034	8843
3838	3843	3884

a) The hundreds digit is 8.

b) The ones digit is one less than the tens digit.

c) The number is 3840 when rounded to the nearest 10.

1 Round these numbers to the nearest 100. You can use the number lines to help you.

a) 10 ☐   b) 70 ☐   c) 43 ☐   d) 50 ☐

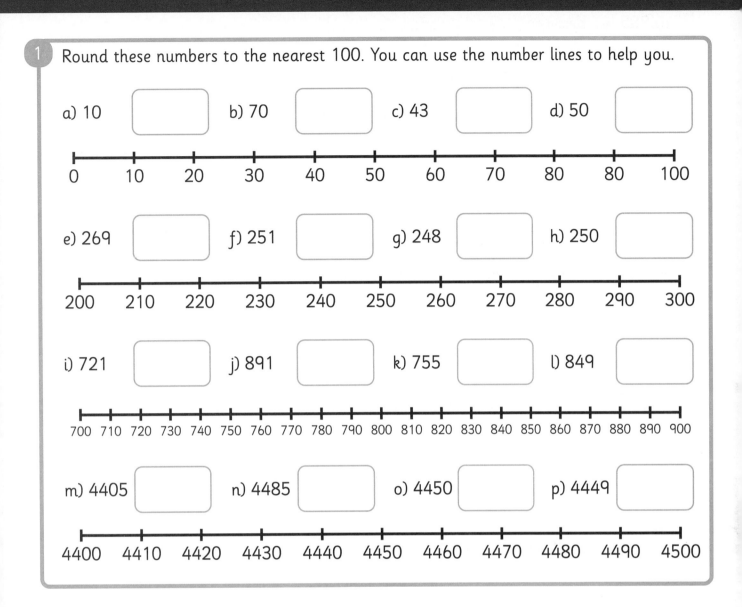

e) 269 ☐   f) 251 ☐   g) 248 ☐   h) 250 ☐

i) 721 ☐   j) 891 ☐   k) 755 ☐   l) 849 ☐

m) 4405 ☐   n) 4485 ☐   o) 4450 ☐   p) 4449 ☐

2 Write the two multiples of 100 on each side of the target numbers and state whether the number is rounded up or down to the nearest 100.

a) 277 lies between ☐ 200 ☐ and ☐ 300 ☐   ☐ rounded up ☐

b) 805 lies between ☐ and ☐   ☐

c) 51 lies between ☐ and ☐   ☐

d) 985 lies between [ ] and [ ]   [ ]

e) 1043 lies between [ ] and [ ]   [ ]

f) 1169 lies between [ ] and [ ]   [ ]

---

3 Are these number sentences true or false? Circle your choice. If false, write the correct rounded estimate in the answer box.

a) 75 rounded to the nearest 100 is **100**.   (True)   False   [ ]

b) 51 rounded to the nearest 100 is **0**.   True   False   [ ]

c) 23 rounded to the nearest 100 is **0**.   True   False   [ ]

d) 655 rounded to the nearest 100 is **600**.   True   False   [ ]

e) 1045 rounded to the nearest 100 is **1000**.   True   False   [ ]

f) 1150 rounded to the nearest 100 is **2000**.   True   False   [ ]

4 Match the numbers on the left to the correct answer on the right when you round to 100.

123	800
55	
769	1000
945	200
844	
149	900
951	100

★ **Challenge**

1. How many numbers would give 500 as an answer when rounded to the nearest hundred?

2. Is this the same number of answers you would get if you were rounding to 600? Why do you think that is?

1 Round these numbers to the nearest whole number. You can use the number lines to help you.

a) 1·2 ☐   b) 1·8 ☐   c) 1·4 ☐   d) 1·5 ☐

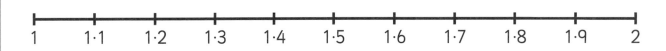

e) 21·8 ☐   f) 20·7 ☐   g) 21·4 ☐   h) 20·5 ☐

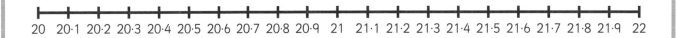

i) 130·9 ☐   j) 131·4 ☐   k) 131·5 ☐   l) 130·1 ☐

2 Which of these decimal fractions would give 150 when rounded to the nearest whole number? Circle them. One has been done for you.

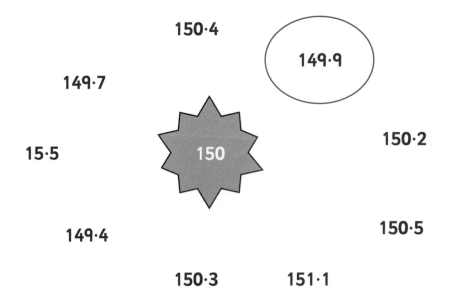

150·4

149·9

149·7

150·2

15·5   150

149·4   150·5

150·3   151·1

3 Below is a table that shows the average monthly rainfall in Inverness and Edinburgh.

Rainfall (mm)	Jan	Feb	Mar	Apr	May	Jun
Inverness	35·2	31·2	30·2	31·8	36·5	47
Edinburgh	51·1	41·1	40·2	39·4	39·6	46·4
Rainfall (mm)	Jul	Aug	Sep	Oct	Nov	Dec
Inverness	52	56·5	50·7	53·4	43·6	36·9
Edinburgh	54·9	58·5	52·9	64·7	57·8	54·6

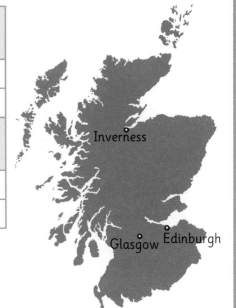

Inverness

Glasgow Edinburgh

a) Round each of these numbers to the nearest whole number and write them in the table below.

Rainfall (mm)	Jan	Feb	Mar	Apr	May	Jun
Inverness						
Edinburgh						
Rainfall (mm)	Jul	Aug	Sep	Oct	Nov	Dec
Inverness						
Edinburgh						

b) Order the months of average rainfall for Inverness from least to most.

Rainfall (mm)	LEAST					
Inverness						
Rainfall (mm)						MOST
Inverness						

c) In Inverness, which month has the least rainfall? Which has the most?

d) Order the months of average rainfall for Edinburgh from least to most. Which month has the least? Which has the most?

Rainfall (mm)	**LEAST**					
Edinburgh						
Rainfall (mm)						**MOST**
Edinburgh						

e) Why do you think your answers for c) and d) have differences?

1. This is the average monthly rainfall for Glasgow. Round the decimal fractions to the nearest whole number then make a bar chart to show this information.

   Remember to label the axes!

Rainfall (mm)	Jan	Feb	Mar	Apr	May	Jun
Glasgow	95·9	77·6	69·1	55	54·6	60·2
Rainfall (mm)	Jul	Aug	Sep	Oct	Nov	Dec
Glasgow	70·8	80·3	81·9	99·9	95·5	97·7

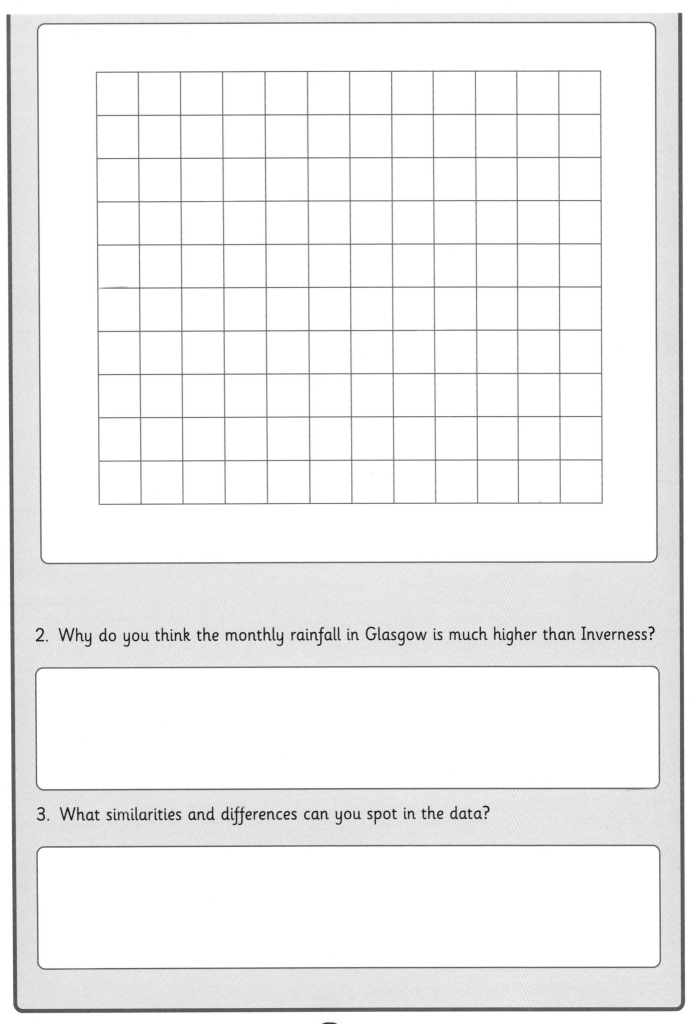

2. Why do you think the monthly rainfall in Glasgow is much higher than Inverness?

3. What similarities and differences can you spot in the data?

1.4 Estimating the answer using rounding

1 Estimate the answer to these questions by rounding to the nearest 10.

a) 24 + 33 [ ]   b) 27 + 51 [ ]   c) 25 + 49 [ ]

d) 46 + 52 [ ]   e) 53 + 64 [ ]   f) 117 + 42 [ ]

g) 123 + 55 [ ]   h) 138 + 87 [ ]

2 Estimate the answer to these questions by rounding to the nearest 10.

a) 34 – 13 [ ]   b) 57 – 29 [ ]   c) 95 – 32 [ ]

d) 142 – 23 [ ]   e) 123 – 62 [ ]   f) 175 – 102 [ ]

g) 229 – 57 [ ]   h) 335 – 207 [ ]

3 Finlay has been practising rounding to the nearest 10 to help him estimate answers to calculations. Which are correct? Put a ✔ next to the ones that are right and correct the ones that are wrong.

a) 205 + 112   is approximately   210 + 100 = 310   [ ]   [ ]

b) 397 – 202   is approximately   400 – 210 = 610   [ ]   [ ]

c) 255 + 175   is approximately   250 + 170 = 420   [ ]   [ ]

d) 406 – 189   is approximately   400 – 200 = 200   [ ]   [ ]

Amman, Finlay, Isla and Nuria all went out for dinner. Explain whether their estimates are reasonable or not. If not, where do you think they went wrong?

Amman

"I had soup, burger and chips, and apple crumble and custard. I think my bill will be about £19."

Finlay

"I had garlic bread, macaroni cheese and sticky toffee pudding. I think my bill will be about £19."

Isla

"I had soup, fish and chips, and sticky toffee pudding. I think my bill will be about £21."

Nuria

"I had garlic bread, fish and chips, and apple crumble and custard. I think my bill will be about £19."

Menu

Starters
Soup - £3.95
Garlic bread - £3.45

Mains
Burger & chips - £12.55
Macaroni cheese - £10.95
Fish & chips - £11.85

Desserts
Sticky toffee pudding - £4.75
Apple crumble & custard - £4.45

2.1 Reading and writing whole numbers

1 Write these numbers in numerals on the blank place value houses below.

a) Three thousand, five hundred and twenty-four.

Thousands		Ones		
	O	H	T	O

b) Two thousand, four hundred and sixty-two.

Thousands		Ones		
	O	H	T	O

c) Five thousand, eight hundred and eighty-seven.

Thousands		Ones		
	O	H	T	O

d) Nine thousand, nine hundred and ninety-nine.

Thousands		Ones		
	O	H	T	O

2 Write the number shown on each place value house in words.

Describe the position of the place holder in the numbers you have written.

Thousands		Ones		
	O	H	T	O
	9	4	5	0

The place holder is in the _____ position.

Thousands		Ones		
	O	H	T	O
	9	7	0	4

The place holder is in the _____ position.

Thousands		Ones		
	O	H	T	O
	9	0	4	5

The place holder is in the _____ position.

Thousands		Ones		
	O	H	T	O
	9	0	0	5

The place holders are in the _____ and _____ positions.

★ **Challenge**

The children are each given the numeral cards 0, 2, 4 and 9 and asked to make a four-digit number.

1. Isla's number has a 4 in the thousands place and a 2 in the tens place. What could her number be? How many different numbers can she make?

2. Amman's number is bigger than Isla's and has a 4 in the hundreds place. What could his number be? How many different numbers can he make?

3. Nuria's number has a 0 in the tens place and is an odd number. What could her number be? How many different numbers can she make?

2.2 Representing and describing whole numbers

1 Write the number represented by each set of base 10 blocks in numerals and in words.

a)

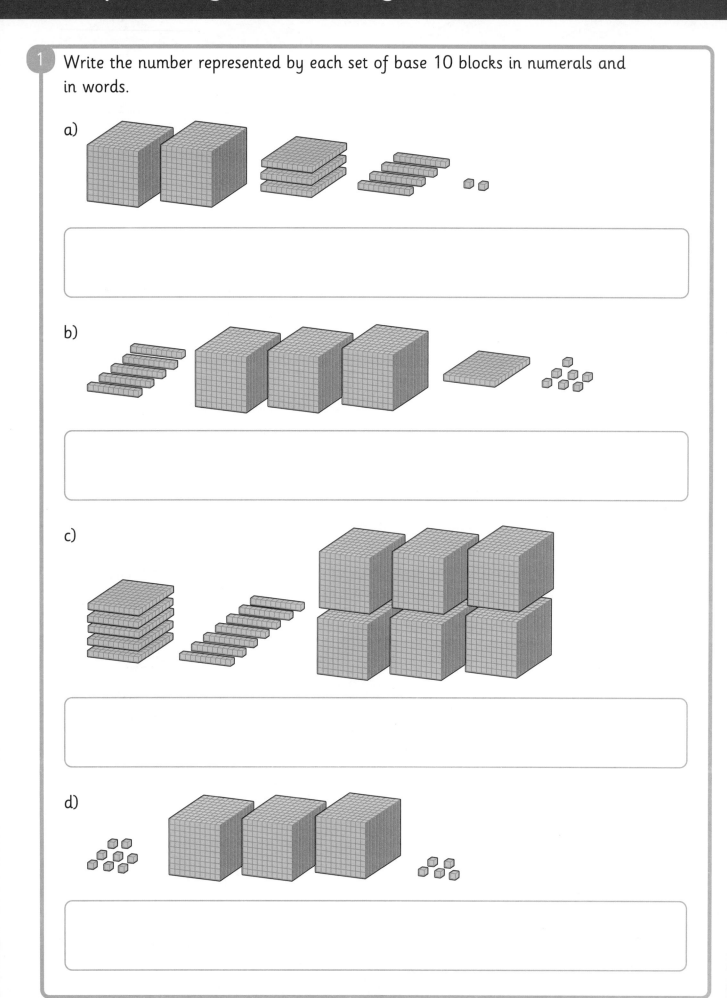

b)

c)

d)

2 Colour the correct number of place value blocks to show the following numbers.

a) 2430

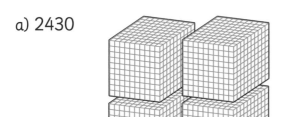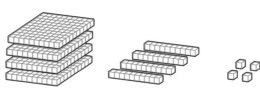

b) 1302

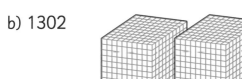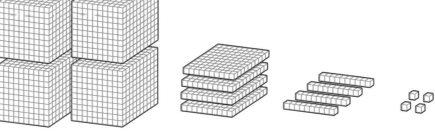

c) 3024

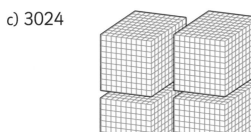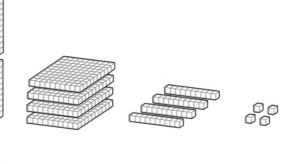

d) 4003

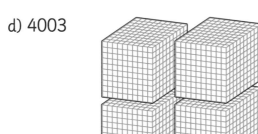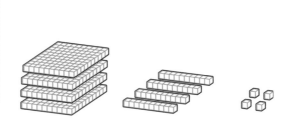

3 Write the numbers you have made above, in words.

a) _____

b) _____

c) _____

d) _____

1. Isla has made a four-digit number with her base ten blocks. She has a combination of thousands, hundreds, tens and ones. She has five of one type of block, six of another type, seven of another type and a place holder. What numbers could Isla have made?

2. Amman has also made a four-digit number. He has eight of one type of block, nine of another and two place holders. What numbers could Amman have made?

3. Order the numbers that Isla and Amman could have made from smallest to largest.

1 Write the number shown by these place value houses in words and in numerals. Partition the number using standard place value partitioning. The first one has been done for you.

a)

Thousands		Ones		
	O	H	T	O
	2	3	4	5

2345 = 2 thousands, 3 hundreds, 4 tens and 5 ones.

2000 + 300 + 40 + 5

b)

Thousands		Ones		
	O	H	T	O
	2	3	4	9

c)

Thousands		Ones		
	O	H	T	O
	2	3	6	9

d)

Thousands		Ones		
	O	H	T	O
	2	5	6	9

e)

Thousands		Ones		
	O	H	T	O
	8	5	6	9

2 a) Match each number up with the different ways to make it.

i) 340

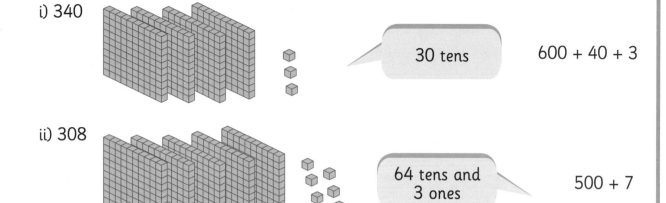

30 tens

600 + 40 + 3

ii) 308

64 tens and 3 ones

500 + 7

iii) 300

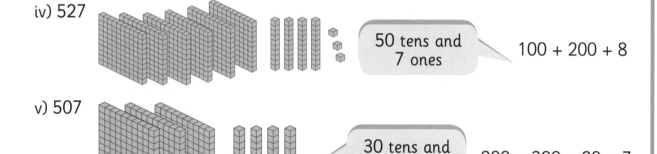

3 hundreds and 40 ones

200 + 200 + 3

iv) 527

50 tens and 7 ones

100 + 200 + 8

v) 507

30 tens and 8 ones

200 + 300 + 20 + 7

vi) 643

4 hundreds and 3 ones

100 + 200 + 20 + 20

vii) 403

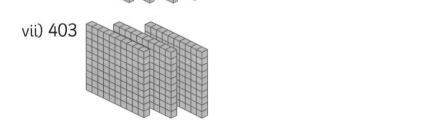

b) Two of the above numbers are only made in two different ways, not three.

Write the three different ways you can make these numbers below.

22

3 Amman makes the number 3450 using place value arrow cards. He can partition this in two ways: 3 thousands, 4 hundreds, 5 tens and 0 ones **OR** 3 thousands, 4 hundreds and 50 ones.

| 3 | 4 | 5 | 0 |

3 thousands, 4 hundreds, 5 tens and 0 ones
3 thousands, 4 hundreds and 50 ones

Partition the following numbers in two ways.

a) | 3 | 4 | 0 | 5 |

b) | 5 | 0 | 3 | 4 |

c) | 4 | 5 | 3 | 0 |

d) | 4 | 0 | 0 | 3 |

★ **Challenge**

How many different ways can you show the number 7604? Consider using: place value houses, arrow cards, base ten blocks, numerals and words. Draw or write them in the box below.

2.4 Comparing and ordering numbers in the range 0 – 10 000

1 Write each of these sets of numbers in order from smallest to largest.

a) 1324   24   324   _____   _____   _____

b) 2324   1324   4324   _____   _____   _____

c) 5670   5607   5067   _____   _____   _____

d) 9008   9090   9009   _____   _____   _____

2 Use these digit cards.

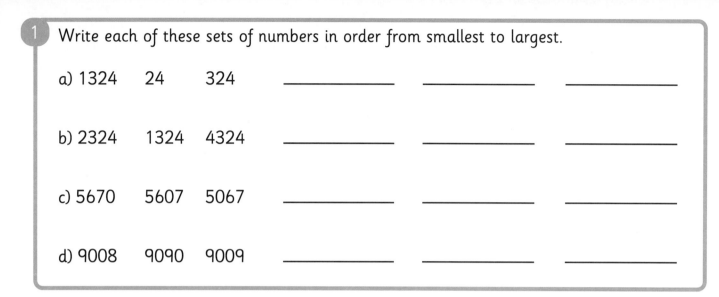

a) How many different numbers between 3000 and 6000 can you make?

b) Write them in order from smallest to largest.

3 Write a number in each of the boxes which will order the sets of numbers from largest to smallest.

a) 7850   7840   [   ]   7820   [   ]

b) 7750   [   ]   7650   [   ]   7550

c) [   ]   7100   [   ]   7080   [   ]

d) 7100   [   ]   7010   [   ]   6900

★ Challenge

Amman and Isla each pick 4 four-digit number cards from the cards shown.

2642   3042   2462   3402

2246   2264   3204   2426

1. Amman organises his numbers in increasing order. Isla orders hers in decreasing order. How might Amman and Isla have ordered their cards?

Amman: _____   _____   _____   _____

Isla: _____   _____   _____   _____

2. Amman now picks a new group of cards and puts them in ascending order. Isla takes the remaining cards and puts them in ascending order. Isla notices that her first card is bigger than Amman's but the last number is smaller than his. Which cards did they each pick?

[   ]

2.5 Reading and writing decimal fractions

1 We can write this decimal fraction in three ways:

 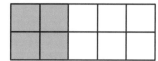

$\underline{\qquad 1{\cdot}4 \qquad}$ $\underline{\qquad \frac{14}{10} \qquad}$ $\underline{\text{one point four}}$

Write the decimal fraction shown by each diagram in three different ways.

a) 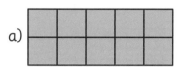  _____ _____ _____

b)   _____ _____ _____

c)  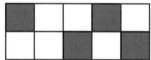 _____ _____ _____

d) 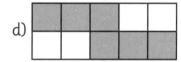 _____ _____ _____

e) 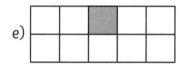 _____ _____ _____

f)  _____ _____ _____

2 Find the matching amounts.

a) Write **a** next to all the representations that match three point six.

b) Write **b** next to all the representations that match two point four.

c) Write **c** next to all the representations that match zero point eight.

d) Write **d** next to all the representations that match four point five.

e) Write **e** next to all the representations that match the '**mystery number**'.

0·8	three point six
4·5	two point four
2·4	zero point eight
1·9	four point five

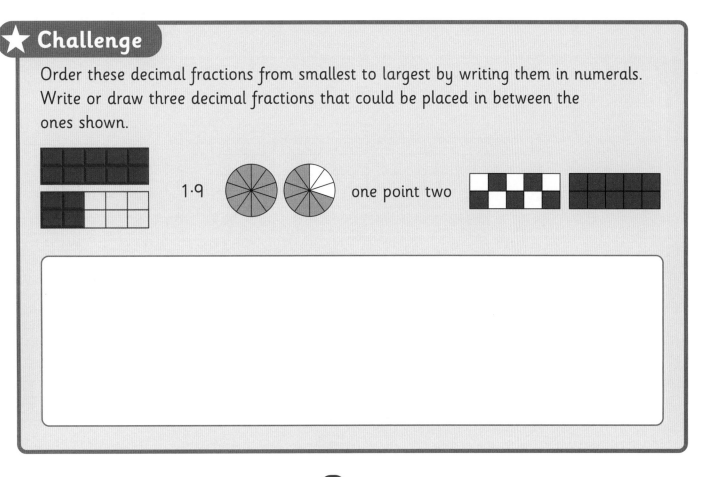

★ Challenge

Order these decimal fractions from smallest to largest by writing them in numerals. Write or draw three decimal fractions that could be placed in between the ones shown.

1·9   one point two

2.6 Representing and describing decimal fractions

1 The decimal fraction 1·2 has 1 whole and 2 tenths or 12 tenths.

Fill in the blanks to show how these decimal fractions can be written.

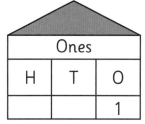

a) 1·4 = _____ whole and _____ tenths = _____ tenths

b) 2·9 = _____ = _____ tenths

c) 3·9 = _____ = _____ tenths

d) 0·7 = _____ = _____ tenths

e) 15·7 = _____ = _____ tenths

2 Colour the models to show the following decimal fractions. State how many tenths there are.

a) 1·8

[ ] tenths

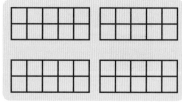
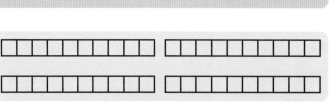

b) 2·4

[ ] tenths

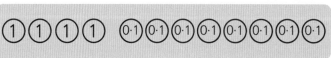
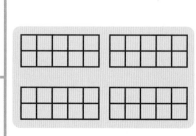
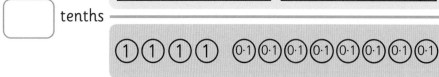

c) 0·4

☐ tenths

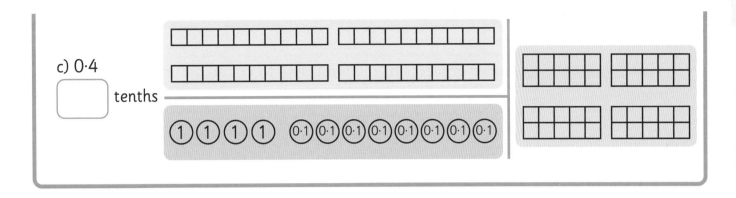

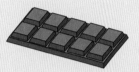

★ Challenge

Finlay, Isla and Nuria share this bar of chocolate.

Is there enough chocolate for all four children? Explain your thinking.

> I'd like six tenths of it but I will save three tenths of my share for Amman so he doesn't miss out.

> I'd like 0·3 of the chocolate.

> I'm still a bit full from lunch, so I'd just like one square.

2.7 Comparing and ordering decimal fractions

1 Colour the correct number of pieces of the ten frame to create an accurate number line.

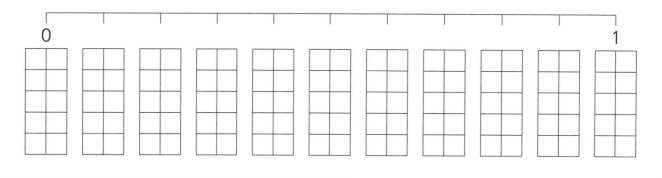

2 Write the decimal fractions that are missing from these number lines.

a)

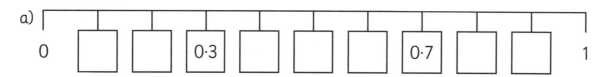

0   ☐   ☐   0·3   ☐   ☐   ☐   0·7   ☐   ☐   1

b)

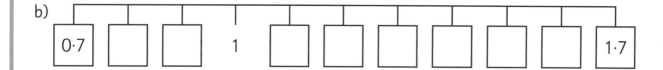

0·7   ☐   ☐   1   ☐   ☐   ☐   ☐   ☐   ☐   1·7

c)

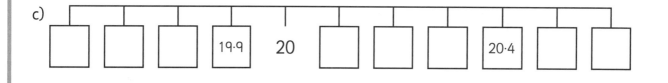

☐   ☐   ☐   19·9   20   ☐   ☐   ☐   20·4   ☐   ☐

3 Choose the correct symbol **< >** or **=** to make each statement true.

a) 1·4   ☐

b) 1·9   ☐

c) 1·6   ☐

d) 0·5 ☐

e) 0·7 ☐

f) 0·2 ☐

★ **Challenge**

Amman, Finlay, Isla and Nuria all choose decimal fractions which lie between 9 and 11. All the decimal fractions they choose have a digit which is not zero, in the tenths place.

1. Use the number line to work out what decimal fraction they could each have chosen. Write them on the number line.

```
9                              10                              11
|—|—|—|—|—|—|—|—|—|—|—|—|—|—|—|—|—|—|—|—|
```

Amman says, "My secret number has 102 tenths."

Finlay says, "My secret number is greater than Amman's but less than 10·5."

Isla says, "My secret number is less than Amman's. It has a 6 in the tenths place."

Nuria says, "I have the largest secret number. It has the same number of tenths as Isla's."

2. Use the correct symbol "< > or =" to compare their decimal fractions.

Amman ☐ Finlay   Isla ☐ Amman

Amman ☐ Isla   Isla ☐ Finlay

Amman ☐ Nuria   Isla ☐ Nuria

1 Use the weather map to write the temperature of the cities in three ways. One has been done for you.

a) Inverness:

−11 °C

Eleven degrees below zero

Minus eleven degrees

INVERNESS (−11)

ABERDEEN (−9)

DUNDEE (−7)

STIRLING (−6)

EDINBURGH (−4)

GLASGOW (−3)

b) Aberdeen:

c) Dundee:

d) Stirling:

e) Edinburgh:

f) Glasgow:

2 Finlay did some research on things he might find off the coast of Scotland and drew this diagram. Record the depth above or below sea level for each object in the picture. One has been done for you.

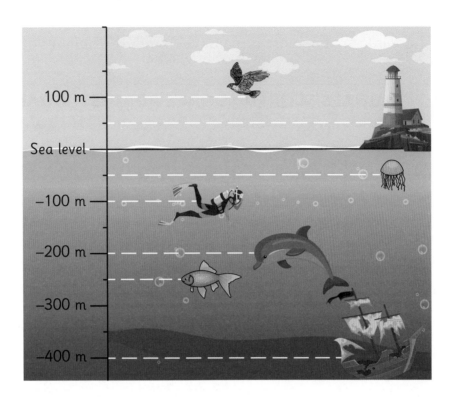

a) 250m below sea level

b) _____

c) _____

d) _____

e) _____

f) _____

g) _____

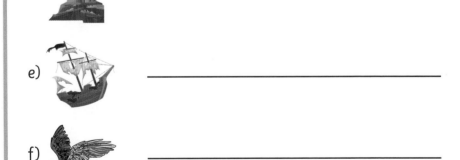

In football, teams get points for winning or drawing matches. The number of goals the teams score and the number of goals that are scored against them are also included in the football tables. To work out the goal difference (GD), we subtract the number of goals scored against a team (GA) from the number of goals the team scored (GS).

TEAM	GOALS SCORED (GS)	GOALS AGAINST (GA)	GOAL DIFFERENCE (GS – GA = GD)
Albion Rovers	47	48	–1
Elgin	44	62	
Forfar	37	43	
East Fife	54	50	
Stranraer	43	57	
Stenhousemuir	51	55	

1. Complete the table to show the Goal Difference.

2. Which team had the most goals scored against them?

3. Which team do you think is top of the table? Explain your choice.

3.1 Mental addition and subtraction of two- and three-digit numbers

1 Use 'round and adjust' to work out the answers to these calculations. The first one has been done for you.

a) $87 - 49 \rightarrow$ $87 - 50 + 1 = 38$

b) $87 - 59 \rightarrow$

c) $59 + 26 \rightarrow$

d) $88 + 26 \rightarrow$

e) $134 + 58 \rightarrow$

f) $258 - 34 \rightarrow$

2 Use 'give and take' to work out the answers to these calculations. The first one has been done for you.

a) $57 + 38 \rightarrow$ $55 + 40 = 95$

b) $87 + 38 \rightarrow$

c) $163 - 57 \rightarrow$

d) 163 − 87 →

e) 125 + 58 →

f) 358 − 34 →

3 State whether you would use 'round and adjust' or 'give and take' to work out the answers to these calculations. Explain why, then use the strategy to calculate the answer.

a) 125 + 39

b) 247 − 63

c) 346 + 76

d) 346 − 68

Amman and Nuria are describing how they used compensation.

> I took 4 from 85 and added it to 136 to make 140.

1. What was Amman's question? What strategy is he using to answer it?

   Write his question and answer it.

> First, I rounded the second number up to 50. I know that 176 minus 50 is 126, but this was taking one too many away, so I added 1 to the answer.

2. What was Nuria's question? What strategy is she using to answer it?

   Write her question and answer it.

3.2 Adding and subtracting 1, 10, 100 and 1000

1 Write the next five numbers in each sequence.

a) 1234, 1235, 1236...

b) 1234, 1233, 1232...

c) 1996, 1997, 1998...

d) 1234, 1244, 1254...

e) 1234, 1224, 1214...

f) 1966, 1976, 1986...

2 What happens when these numbers are entered into the function machines?

Write the number that will come out.

IN   OUT

1959   **+1**

1299

1999

IN   OUT

1740   **−1**

1700

4000

IN   OUT

1740   **+100**

1700

5900

IN   OUT

3840   **−100**

3801

8000

3 Complete the number lines.

a) What numbers are missing from the number line when you jump on 1000 each time?

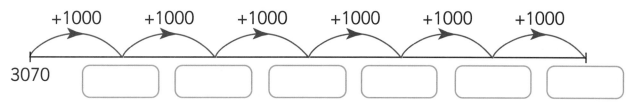

3070

b) What numbers are missing from the number line when you jump back 1000 each time?

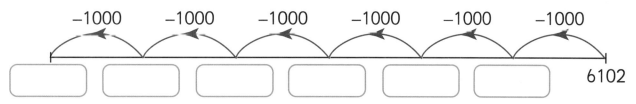

6102

c) What numbers are missing from the number line when you jump on 1000 each time?

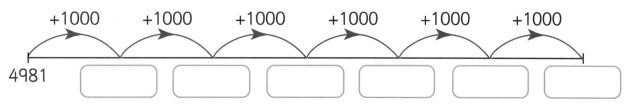

4981

d) What numbers are missing from the number line when you jump back 1000 each time?

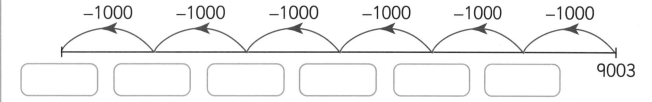

9003

★ **Challenge**

Amman is checking Isla's work but has forgotten to do the last part. Put a ✓ or ✗ to show if they are right or wrong. If wrong, help Isla by writing the correct answer.

a) 10 more than 2000 is 2100. ☐

b) 100 less than 2000 is 2090. ☐

c) 1000 more than 2090 is 3090. ☐

d) 1000 less than 2090 is 1900. ☐

3.3 Adding and subtracting multiples of 100

1 The numbers 700, 200, 100 and 400 are one hundred times bigger than 7, 2, 1 and 4. So 700 + 200 + 100 + 400 = 1400. Complete the patterns and find the missing totals.

a)   4 +   3 +   2 +   5 = [ ]

    400 + [ ] + 200 + [ ] = [ ]

b)   1600 − [ ] − [ ] − 100 = [ ]

    [ ] − 4 − 3 − [ ] = [ ]

c)   5700 + 400 + [ ] + [ ] = [ ]

    [ ] + [ ] + 6 + 13 = [ ]

2 Finlay, Isla and Nuria are playing a ball game. This is where their balls landed.

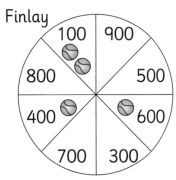

Finlay
100 | 900
800 | 500
400 | 600
700 | 300

Isla
100 | 900
800 | 500
400 | 600
700 | 300

Nuria
100 | 900
800 | 500
400 | 600
700 | 300

a) How many points did they each score?

Finlay [ ]   **Isla** [ ]   **Nuria** [ ]

b) Who scored the most and least points?

c) What is the difference in points between the highest and lowest scores?

d) Find four different ways of scoring exactly 2000 with four balls.

Amman and Isla are playing a card game. They have these cards to choose from and can pick five cards.

| 500 | 1100 | 300 | 800 | 1200 | 200 | 700 |

1. What cards should be picked to make the highest score possible?

2. What cards should be picked to make the second lowest score possible?

3. What is the difference between your answers to questions 1 and 2?

1 Calculate mentally. Look for multiples of 10 or 100. You may find it helpful to jot these numbers down. The first one has been done for you.

Jottings

a) 22 + 534 + 48 = 604   534 + 70 = 500 + 100 + 4

b) 534 + 26 + 48 =

c) 530 + 48 + 70 =

d) 530 + 172 + 48 =

e) 172 + 455 + 28 =

f) 455 + 315 + 145 =

2 Calculate mentally. You may find it helpful to draw or imagine counting on or back on an empty number line and jot down the jumps you make. The first one has been done for you.

Jottings

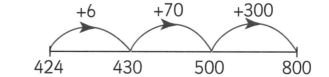

a) 800 – 424 = 376   424   430   500   800

b) 800 – 624 =

c) 600 – 472 =

d) 400 – 235 =

e) 400 – 237 =

f) 400 – 219 =

3 Find the missing number in each of these calculations in only two jumps, by imagining or drawing an empty number line.

Jottings

a) 500 − [ ] = 273

b) [ ] + 273 = 600

c) [ ] − 278 = 522

d) 1000 − 278 = [ ]

★ Challenge

Finlay and Isla are playing a card game. They have to pick pairs of cards which add up to multiples of 10 or 100. Which cards can they pick?

| 225 | 304 | 86 | 75 | 96 | 115 |

3.5 Adding and subtracting multiples of 1000

1 Work out the missing numbers on each number line, then write one addition and one subtraction calculation to match it. One has been done for you.

a)
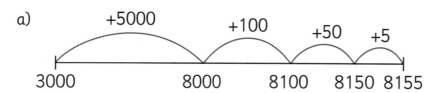

$3000 + 5155 = 8155$
$8155 - 5155 = 3000$

b)
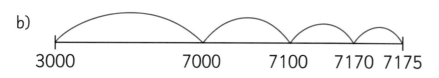

c)
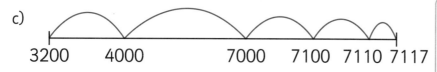

d)
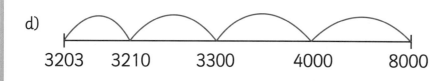

2 Choose between counting on and counting back to solve these problems.

<u>Jottings</u>

a) [ ] $+ 1468 = 9000$

b) $1468 +$ [ ] $= 6000$

c) $6000 =$ [ ] $- 2463$

d) $2475 -$ [ ] $= 6000$

Complete the puzzles by writing a four-digit number in each empty triangle.

Triangles around the outside must total the number in the centre.

Can you find three different answers for triangles 2 and 3?

1.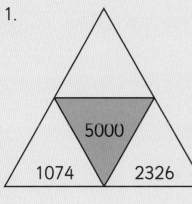

5000

1074   2326

2.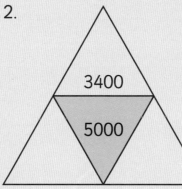

3400

5000

3.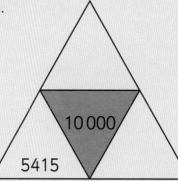

10 000

5415

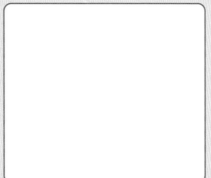

3.6 Adding and subtracting multiples of 10 and 100

1   Use **place value partitioning** to work out these calculations.
The first one has been done for you.

a) 2335 + 190

2000 + 300 + 30 + 5 add 100 + 90
2000 + 300 + 100 + 30 + 90 + 5 = 2000 + 400 + 120 + 5 = 2525

b) 2335 + 790

c) 1790 + 5936

d) 5936 + 2100

e) 2500 + 2877

f) 2877 – 540

g) 2877 – 760

h) 2877 – 1553

i) 7980 – 1403

2 Replace the ⭐ with a multiple of 10 or 100 to make each number sentence true.

a) 3455 + ⭐ = 3955

b) ⭐ + 3455 = 3685

c) 9674 − ⭐ = 9274

d) ⭐ − 760 = 240

⭐ **Challenge**

The answer is 7650. Write three addition and three subtraction calculations that use multiples of 10 and 100 and give 7650 as the answer.

3.7 Solving word problems

Draw a bar model to represent each problem then solve the problem using a strategy of your choice.

1 Dunrobin Castle had 1370 visitors between Monday and Friday and 2440 visitors at the weekend. How many people visited the castle that week? ▢

2 At the castle in the month of April, 1400 people went to the falconry display, 4276 people visited the tearoom and 2624 people visited the museum.

a) How many people is this altogether? ▢

b) Find the difference between the most and least popular attractions at the castle.

3 Of the 2624 people that visited the museum, 1700 of them were children.

How many adults were there? ▢

4 The castle can have 300 visitors in it at once. 128 people are currently inside.

How many more visitors could be allowed in? _____

★ **Challenge**

Write a word problem to match this bar model. Check it makes sense and you have worked out the answer. Ask a friend to solve your word problem. Check their work!

970		
237	496	?

We can draw a Think Board to help us represent and solve a word problem, like this:

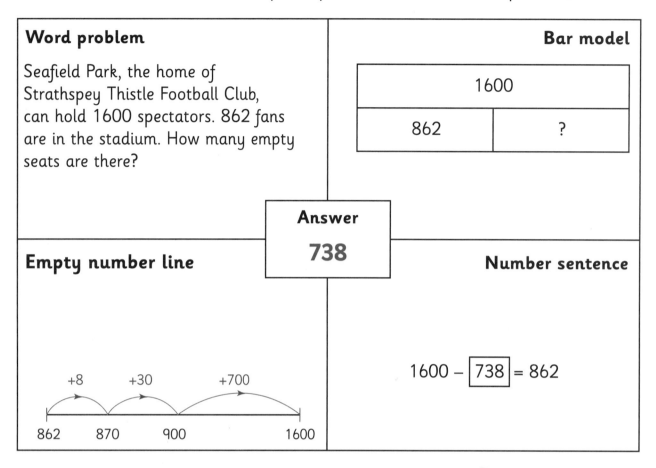

Word problem	Bar model
Seafield Park, the home of Strathspey Thistle Football Club, can hold 1600 spectators. 862 fans are in the stadium. How many empty seats are there?	1600 / 862 ?

Answer

738

Empty number line	Number sentence
+8 +30 +700 / 862 870 900 1600	$1600 - \boxed{738} = 862$

Complete a Think Board to represent and solve each of these word problems.

1

Word problem	Bar model
Fort William Football Club play at Claggan Park, which can hold 4000 spectators. If there are seats for 2768 home fans, how many seats are there for the away spectators?	

Answer

Empty number line	Number sentence

2

Word problem

Bayview Stadium, the home of East Fife FC, can hold 1982 spectators. Find the difference between the number of spectators who can watch football at Claggan Park and Bayview.

Bar model

Answer

Empty number line

Number sentence

3

Word problem

Falkirk Stadium can hold 7937 people in the stands. However, when they host a concert and use the pitch, the capacity increases to 9200.
How many people can watch the concert from the pitch?

Bar model

Answer

Empty number line

Number sentence

Challenge

Write a word problem for this partially completed Think Board.

Complete the Think Board for your word problem.

Word problem	Bar model

	4396	2614

Answer

Empty number line	Number sentence

Workings

3.9 Using non-standard place value partitioning

1 Write the total represented by each set of place value counters in two different ways. One has been done for you.

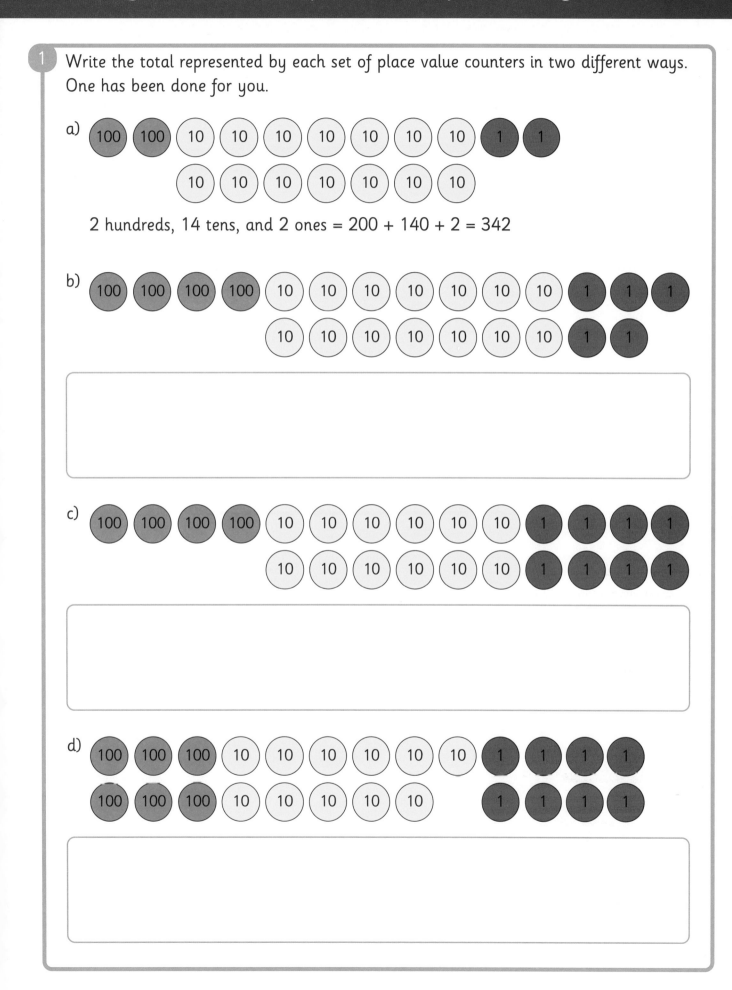

a)

2 hundreds, 14 tens, and 2 ones = 200 + 140 + 2 = 342

b)

c)

d)

2 Create the following numbers in two different ways using the place value counters. Write on the values 100, 10 and 1 as you need them. Remember to group the hundreds, tens and ones. You do not need to use all the counters.

a) 352

b) 653

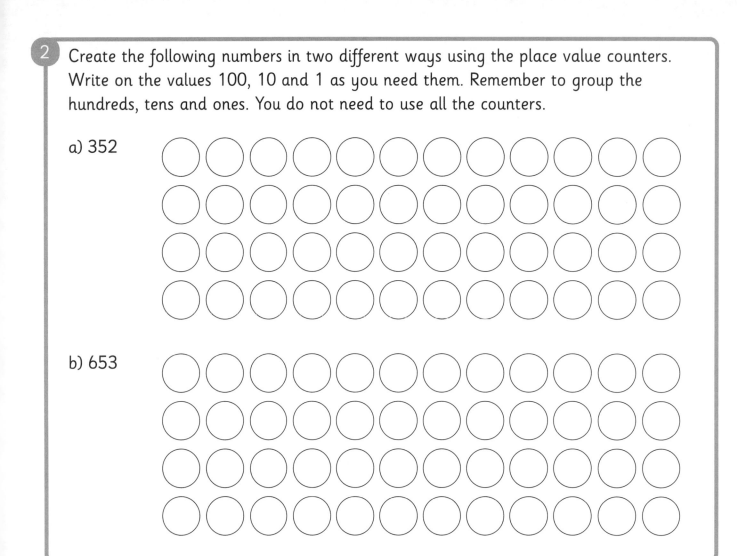

3 Pencils can be bought in boxes of 100 as well as packs of 10 and as singles. Ms MacDonald needs to buy 184 pencils so that every pupil at school has one on their first day. Show four different ways that she could buy 184 pencils. Include a box of 100 each time.

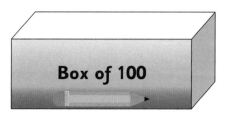

Box of 100

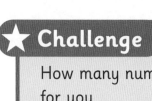

How many numbers can you make with these place value cards? One has been done for you.

2 hundreds	17 ones	5 ones	6 tens	14 tens

265 = 2 hundreds, 6 tens and 5 ones = 200 + 60 + 5

1 Finlay uses the following strategy to add 467 and 275.

467 + 275

```
  600
  130
   12
  ───
  742
```

400 add 200 is 600
60 add 70 is 130
7 add 5 is 12
600 + 130 + 12 = 742

Use Finlay's method to calculate the following.

a) 345 + 252

```
┌─┐┌─┐ ┌─┐
└─┘└─┘ └─┘
┌─┐┌─┐ ┌─┐
└─┘└─┘ └─┘
      ┌─┐┌─┐
   +  └─┘└─┘
   ─────────
┌─┐┌─┐┌─┐
└─┘└─┘└─┘
```

b) 345 + 259

```
┌─┐┌─┐ ┌─┐
└─┘└─┘ └─┘
┌─┐┌─┐ ┌─┐
└─┘└─┘ └─┘
      ┌─┐┌─┐
   +  └─┘└─┘
   ─────────
┌─┐┌─┐┌─┐
└─┘└─┘└─┘
```

c) 345 + 278

```
┌─┐┌─┐ ┌─┐
└─┘└─┘ └─┘
┌─┐┌─┐ ┌─┐
└─┘└─┘ └─┘
      ┌─┐┌─┐
   +  └─┘└─┘
   ─────────
┌─┐┌─┐┌─┐
└─┘└─┘└─┘
```

d) 345 + 557

```
┌─┐┌─┐ ┌─┐
└─┘└─┘ └─┘
┌─┐┌─┐ ┌─┐
└─┘└─┘ └─┘
      ┌─┐┌─┐
   +  └─┘└─┘
   ─────────
┌─┐┌─┐┌─┐
└─┘└─┘└─┘
```

e) 557 + 373

```
┌─┐┌─┐ ┌─┐
└─┘└─┘ └─┘
┌─┐┌─┐ ┌─┐
└─┘└─┘ └─┘
      ┌─┐┌─┐
   +  └─┘└─┘
   ─────────
┌─┐┌─┐┌─┐
└─┘└─┘└─┘
```

f) 473 + 239

```
┌─┐┌─┐ ┌─┐
└─┘└─┘ └─┘
┌─┐┌─┐ ┌─┐
└─┘└─┘ └─┘
      ┌─┐┌─┐
   +  └─┘└─┘
   ─────────
┌─┐┌─┐┌─┐
└─┘└─┘└─┘
```

2 Find the answers to these additions using the column method.

a) 273 + 213 + 414

[column addition grid with blank boxes, + sign]

b) 273 + 223 + 419

[column addition grid with blank boxes, + sign]

c) 273 + 69 + 409

[column addition grid with blank boxes, + sign]

3 Use the numbers on the cards to make each number sentence true.

You may use each card only once.

| 20 | 600 | 50 |

| 500 | 1000 |

| 70 | 200 |

a) 4258 + [ ] − [ ] = 4838

b) 4258 − [ ] + [ ] = 3308

c) 4258 + [ ] − [ ] + [ ] = 4028

★ **Challenge**

A palindrome is a number that reads the same forwards and backwards, for example 797. Find the missing digit so that each total is a palindrome.

1. 400 + ☆60 + 7 [ ]

2. 400 + ☆50 + 9 [ ]

3. ☆00 + 420 + 9 [ ]

4. ☆00 + ☆70 + 110 + 19 [ ]

1 Write each calculation as a column addition. Use a standard written algorithm to find the answer. One has been done for you.

a) 235 + 386

$$\begin{array}{r} {\scriptstyle 1\ 1} \\ 3\ 8\ 6 \\ +\ 2\ 3\ 5 \\ \hline 6\ 2\ 1 \end{array}$$

b) 235 + 423

c) 235 + 608

d) 235 + 687

e) 687 + 312

f) 687 + 241

g) 687 + 254

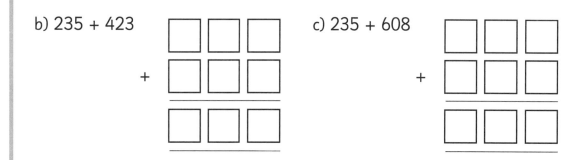

2 Calculate the answers to these questions using the standard written algorithm for addition.

a) 324 + 203 + 160

```
  ☐ ☐ ☐
  ☐ ☐ ☐
+ ☐ ☐ ☐
─────────
  ☐ ☐ ☐
─────────
```

b) 203 + 324 + 156

```
  ☐ ☐ ☐
  ☐ ☐ ☐
+ ☐ ☐ ☐
─────────
  ☐ ☐ ☐
─────────
```

c) 88 + 203 + 314

```
  ☐ ☐ ☐
  ☐ ☐ ☐
+ ☐ ☐ ☐
─────────
  ☐ ☐ ☐
─────────
```

d) 388 + 203 + 375

```
  ☐ ☐ ☐
  ☐ ☐ ☐
+ ☐ ☐ ☐
─────────
  ☐ ☐ ☐
─────────
```

3 Create a complete addition calculation that meets these rules then solve it.

a) Carry one ten over into the tens column.

```
    4 2 5
+   ☐ ☐ ☐
─────────

─────────
```

b) Carry one hundred over into the hundreds column.

```
    4 2 5
+   ☐ ☐ ☐
─────────

─────────
```

c) Carry over both a ten and a hundred.

$$
\begin{array}{r}
4\ \ 2\ \ 5 \\
+\ \square\ \square\ \square \\
\hline
\end{array}
$$

d) Check and complete the calculations you have written.

Part a) checked

Part b) checked

Part c) checked

★ **Challenge**

Paint has been spilled on these calculations! Copy and fill in the missing digits.

$$
\begin{array}{r}
3\ 5\ \text{✱} \\
+\ \text{✱}\ 8\ 2 \\
\hline
6\ \text{✱}\ 9 \\
\end{array}
\qquad
\begin{array}{r}
\text{✱}\ 0\ 9 \\
+\ 7\ \text{✱}\ 7 \\
\hline
1\ 1\ 4\ \text{✱} \\
\end{array}
$$

60

3.12 Representing and solving word problems

We can use bar models, empty number lines, partitioning numbers into hundreds, tens and ones and standard written algorithms to think about, model and solve problems.

Represent and solve these word problems using a method of your choice.

1 Nuria and her family are touring Scotland. They travel 123 miles on Wednesday and 154 miles on Thursday. When they reach Ullapool on Thursday, they have travelled 489 miles. How far did they travel on Thursday?

2 On Friday and Saturday they were exploring the hills around Ullapool. On Friday, they walked up Ullapool Hill (233m) and on Saturday they hiked up Stac Pollaidh (Stac Polly) (612m). How much higher is Stac Pollaidh than Ullapool Hill?

3 Nuria and her family take the ferry to Stornoway. The ferry covers 53 miles. It's another 48 miles to where they are spending the night in Luskentyre. How far will they have travelled during their whole trip when they reach Luskentyre?

4 Luskentyre beach was voted the 'Best Beach in Scotland' in a poll. It received 375 votes the first week of the poll and 586 votes the second week. How many votes did it get in total?

5 Next they visit the statue of Hercules the Bear, a trained grizzly bear who starred in television and films. Hercules went missing in Benbecula in 1980 while filming a television commercial. Volunteers and search parties searched for him for 96 hours but didn't find him. Hercules was spotted swimming in a loch by a local man on the other side of the island 482 hours later. How long was Hercules on his own?

★ Challenge

1. Write two addition number sentences and two subtraction number sentences to fit this bar model.

805		
202	76	527

2. Choose one of your number sentences and write a word problem to match it.

Recalling multiplication and division facts means knowing them straight away.

1 Can you recall these multiplication facts within one minute? Say the fact out loud and then write it in the box. Time yourself!

a) 2 × 7 ☐   b) 5 × 3 ☐   c) 4 × 10 ☐   d) 9 × 2 ☐

e) 5 × 5 ☐   f) 10 × 7 ☐   g) 2 × 8 ☐   h) 7 × 5 ☐

2 Multiply these numbers by 2, then 5 and finally 10.

a) 3 ☐ ☐ ☐

b) 8 ☐ ☐ ☐

c) 9 ☐ ☐ ☐

d) 6 ☐ ☐ ☐

3 Write the number covered by the paint splash.

a) ✷ × 2 = 12 ☐   b) 5 × ✷ = 30 ☐   c) 6 × 10 = ✷ ☐

d) ✷ ÷ 2 = 8 ☐   e) 40 ÷ ✷ = 4 ☐   f) 40 ÷ ✷ = 8 ☐

g) 10 × ✷ = 100 ☐   h) 9 × ✷ = 18 ☐   i) 5 × ✷ = 45 ☐

j) ✷ ÷ 5 = 10 ☐   k) ✷ ÷ 10 = 5 ☐   l) 14 ÷ 2 = ✷ ☐

1. Work out how this multiplication wheel has been completed.

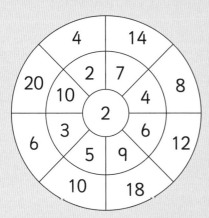

This multiplication wheel has the rule:

2. Insert the missing numbers and find the rule for this multiplication wheel.

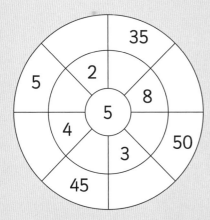

This multiplication wheel has the rule:

3. Isla has drawn this mobile puzzle for Amman to solve. What value does each

⬤ and ▽ have?

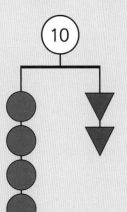

Recalling multiplication and division facts means knowing them straight away.

1

a) What do you multiply by 3 to get 27?

b) $15 \div 3 =$

c) What is 7 times 3?

d) 18 divided by 3 =

e) $7 \times \boxed{} = 21$

f) Nine children split themselves into three equal groups.

How many children in each group?

g) $3 \times 0 =$

h) What do you multiply by 3 to get 24?

i) $12 \div 3 =$

j) How many threes are in 3?

2 Use your knowledge of multiplication facts to complete these triangles. The first one has been done for you.

a)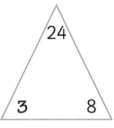

b)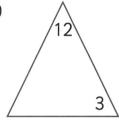

c)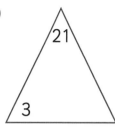

d)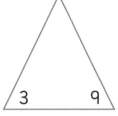

e)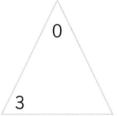

f)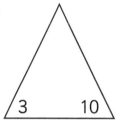

3 Write two multiplication and two division facts for each triangle above. The first one has been done for you.

a) $3 \times 8 = 24$, $8 \times 3 = 24$, $24 \div 3 = 8$, $24 \div 8 = 3$

b)

c)

d)

e)

f)

★ Challenge

1. Complete this 3 Times Table Crossword. All of the calculations are part of the 3 times table. One number or symbol can be inserted into one box.

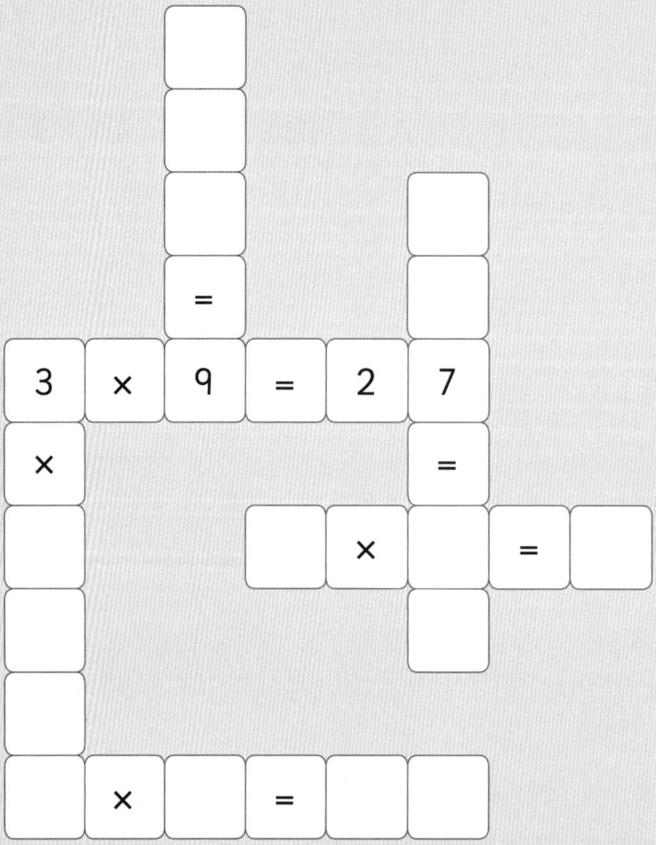

2. Now, make up your own times table crossword for a partner to complete.

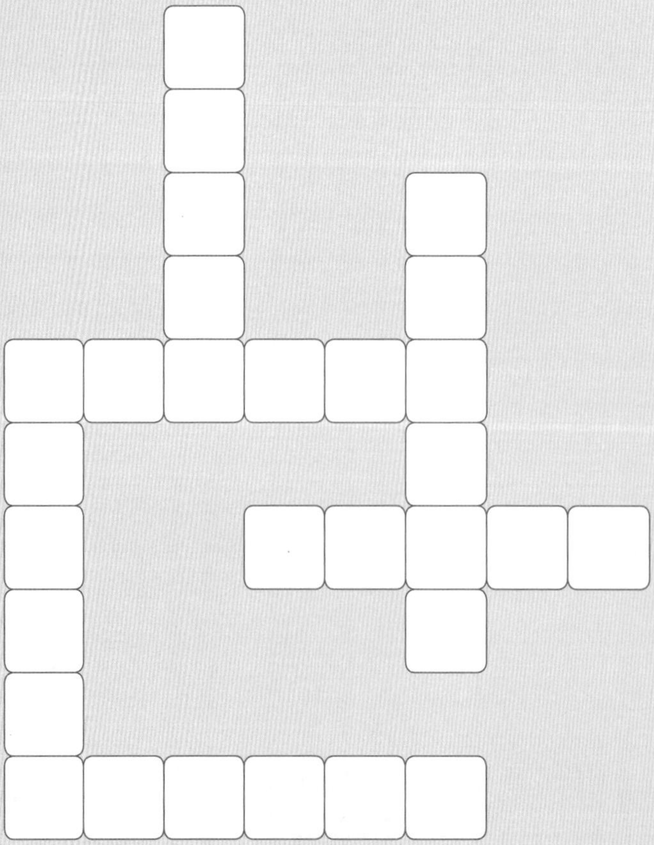

1 Squared paper has been used to make an array for 8 × 7. We can use our 5 and 2 times tables facts to find and represent the answer to 8 × 7.

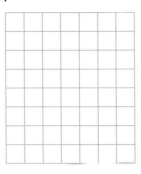

a) What is the answer to 8 × 5? Colour 8 × 5 on your array.

b) What is the answer to 8 × 2? Colour 8 × 2 on your array.

c) Now add your answers together to work out 8 × 7.

d) (8 × 5) + (8 × 2) = _____ + _____ = _____

2 A chocolate bar has nine rows of seven squares. Use 2x and 5x facts to help you work out how many squares altogether. You may wish to use the squared paper to draw an array.

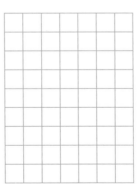

Record your calculation using brackets to show how you split up and grouped your problem.

(_____ × _____) + (_____ × _____) = _____ + _____ = _____

3 How could you use 2×, 5× or 10× facts to help you work out these multiplication problems?

Draw arrays to help you. Use brackets to record your calculations.

a) 6 × 7

(___ × ___) + (___ × ___)

= [   ]

b) 4 × 6

(___ × ___) + (___ × ___)

[   ]

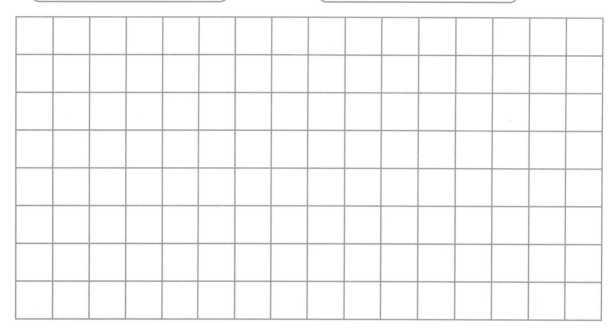

c) 7 × 4

(___ × ___) + (___ × ___)

= [   ]

d) 11 × 7

(___ × ___) + (___ × ___)

[   ]

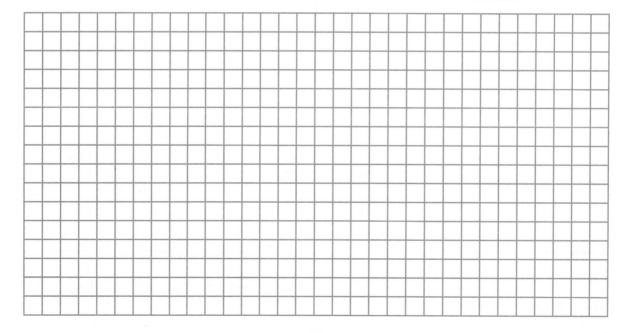

e) 12 × 6

(___ × ___) + (___ × ___)

= [   ]

f) 7 × 15

(___ × ___) + (___ × ___)

[   ]

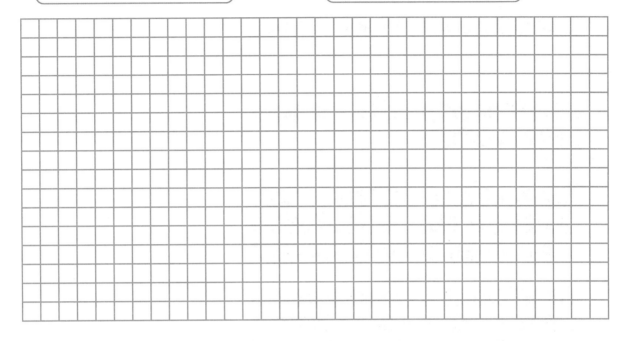

Below is an array of a calculation.

1. Record the calculation using brackets, showing how the array has been split up.

2. What calculation is the array representing?

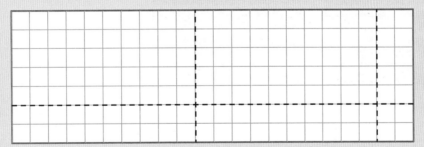

1 Write the multiplication statement that can be made from each of these pictures:

a)

b)

c)

d)

e)

2 Write a multiplication statement to show what each of the following numbers will be when they have been multiplied by 100.

a) 4

b) 8

c) 9

d) 12

e) 22

f) 45

3 There are 100cm in a metre (m). How many centimetres are there in each of the following lengths?

a) 4m [ ]　　b) 8m [ ]　　c) 9m [ ]

d) 14m [ ]　　e) 24m [ ]　　f) 56m [ ]

★ Challenge

1. Match each mobile to the number they represent and the correct multiplication calculation.

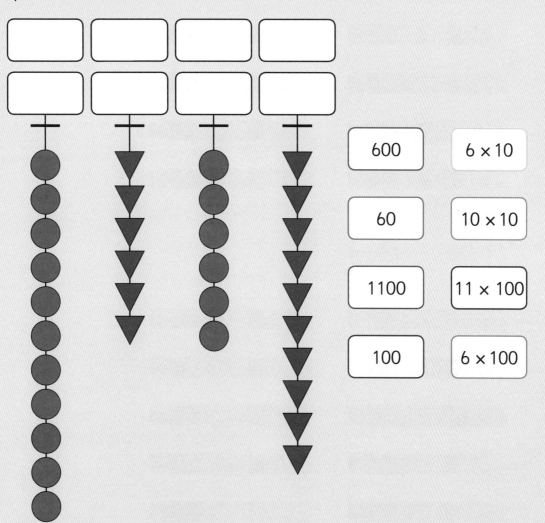

600	6 × 10
60	10 × 10
1100	11 × 100
100	6 × 100

2. What is the value of each ●? [ ]

3. What is the value of each ▼? [ ]

1 Divide each quantity by 10 then write a division number sentence to match the picture. One has been done for you.

a) 20  $20 \div 10 = 2$

b) 40

c) 80

d) 10

e) 100

f) 120

---

2 Divide each of these numbers by 10. Write a division number sentence for each answer.

a)  **30** b)  **70** c)  **90** d) **110** e) **150**

---

3 Paperclips are sold in boxes of 100.

How many boxes would there be if there were:

Box of 100

a) 200 paperclips

b) 500 paperclips

c) 100 paperclips

d) 1000 paperclips

e) 1200 paperclips

f) 1600 paperclips

4 Write multiplication and division number sentences, involving both 10 and 100, for these numbers. One has been done for you.

a) 300: 3 × 100 = 300 and 30 × 10 = 300   300 ÷ 3 = 100 and 300 ÷ 100 = 3

b) 700

c) 1000

d) 1400

e) 2500

★ **Challenge**

Solve these clues to discover the mystery number.

1.  When you divide me by 10, the answer is 20.

2.  When you divide me by 100, the answer is 23.

3.  When you divide me by 10, the answer is 85.

4.  When you divide me by 100, the answer is 99.

1 Amman partitions two-digit numbers into tens and ones using ten frames, to make solving multiplication calculations easier. He then uses brackets to show how he partitioned the problem.

a) What is 16 multiplied by 3?

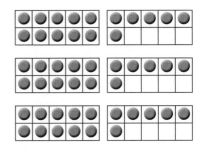

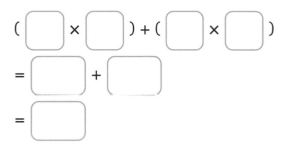

b) Four classes are going to the museum on a school trip. There are 27 pupils in each class. How many tickets need to be bought for pupils?

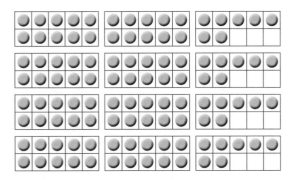

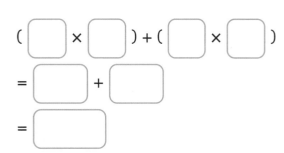

c) Isla's Mum wants to buy three framed photos as a gift. Each framed photo costs £37. How much does she spend on the gifts?

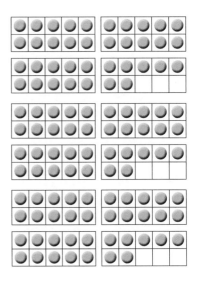

(☐ × ☐) + (☐ × ☐)

= ☐ + ☐

= ☐

2 Use the blank ten frames to show how you would partition these problems.

a) Finlay buys five packs of sweets. There are 35 sweets in each packet. How many sweets does he have altogether?

b) Nuria is making bracelets for herself and three friends. She needs 34 beads for one bracelet. How many beads does she need to be able to finish all the bracelets?

Write a word problem that matches the number statement 32 × 4, then solve it.

Use the blank ten frames to show your working. Include using brackets to record how you solved it.

4.7 Solving multiplication and division problems

We can use doubling and halving to help us solve mental calculations quickly.

1 Double these numbers. Then use the patterns you spot when numbers are ten times bigger to complete the next set of doubles. The first one has been done for you.

a) Double 8 = [16], so double [80] = [160]

b) Double 5 = [ ], so double [ ] = [ ]

c) Double 9 = [ ], so double [ ] = [ ]

e) Double 13 = [ ], so double [ ] = [ ]

f) Double 15 = [ ], so double [ ] = [ ]

2 Halve these numbers. Then use the patterns you spot when numbers are ten times bigger to complete the next set of doubles. The first has been done for you.

a) Half of 8 = [4], so half of [80] = [40]

b) Half of 12 = [ ], so half of [ ] = [ ]

c) Half of 20 = [ ], so half of [ ] = [ ]

d) Half of 50 = [ ], so half of [ ] = [ ]

e) Half of 100 = [ ], so half of [ ] = [ ]

3 These function machines double or halve numbers. The output number has been given. Now write the numbers that have been put into the machines.

⇨ IN   ⇨ OUT   ⇨ IN   ⇨ OUT

	Double			**Half**	
		14			12
		30			20
		66			24

⭐ **Challenge**

1. A toy store has 88 toys on display. Half of the toys are stuffed animals. Half of the stuffed animals are teddy bears. Half of the teddy bears are brown. How many brown teddy bears are there?

2. Now write a halving puzzle for a partner to solve.

1 Use this empty number line to skip-count in fours. Show your skip counting jumps above the line and write the multiples of 4 below the line.

0

2 Use the hundred square to help you answer these questions.

1	2	3	4	5	6	7	8	9	10
11	12	13	14	15	16	17	18	19	20
21	22	23	24	25	26	27	28	29	30
31	32	33	34	35	36	37	38	39	40
41	42	43	44	45	46	47	48	49	50
51	52	53	54	55	56	57	58	59	60
61	62	63	64	65	66	67	68	69	70
71	72	73	74	75	76	77	78	79	80
81	82	83	84	85	86	87	88	89	90
91	92	93	94	95	96	97	98	99	100

a) What are six groups of 4?

b) How many fours are there in 32?

c) What are nine 4s?

d) How many groups of 4 make 16?

e) What are ten 4s?

3 Match each question with the correct answer.

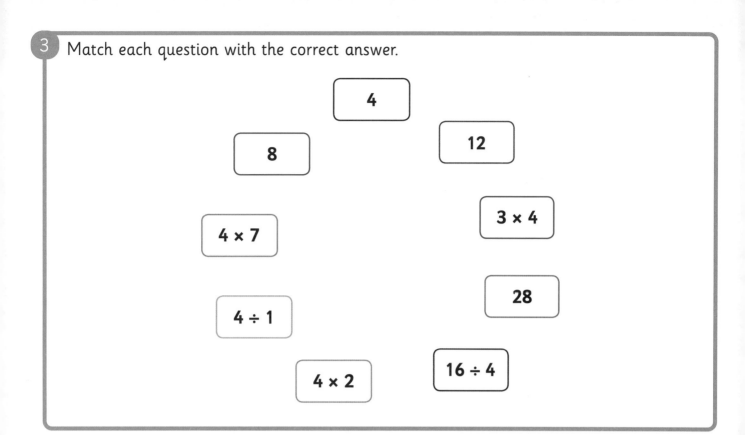

4

8

12

4 × 7

3 × 4

4 ÷ 1

28

4 × 2

16 ÷ 4

⭐ **Challenge**

Isla and her three friends make £60 from selling the bracelets they made. How much money do they each get once this has been shared equally between the four of them?

Record how you worked out the problem.

4.9 Solving division problems

1 The teacher gives Nuria's group 32 cards to share between herself and the three others in her group. How many cards does each group member get?

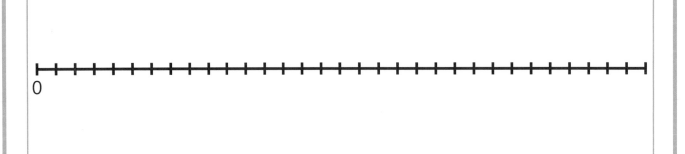

0

2 How many groups of five pencils can be made with 25 pencils?

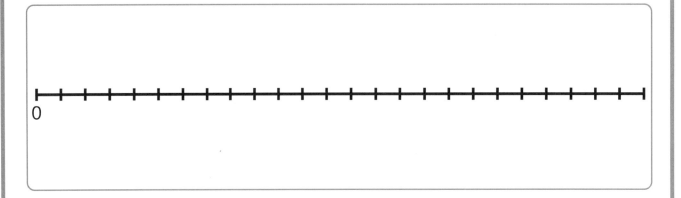

0

3 At the School Fair, Amman is in charge of making sure each stall has change at the beginning of the day. He has £84 in change to share between the 12 stalls. How much change does each stall get?

0

4 At the Cake and Candy stall, Finlay and Isla are in charge of making bags of tablet to sell. They need to put six squares of tablet in each bag. There are 78 squares of tablet altogether. How many bags can they make?

0 |——————————————————————————————————————|

★ **Challenge**

At the Primary 5 party, there are 64 children. For playing games, they need to be split into equal groups, so no one is left out. What different sized groups can be made?

0 |——————————————————————————————————————|

When we multiply numbers, it doesn't matter what order the factors are in:

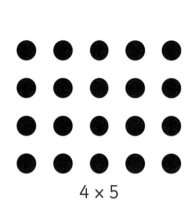

4 × 5

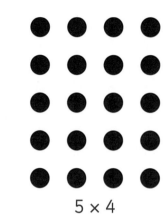

5 × 4

1   Use the squared paper to help you draw arrays for these multiplication sentences. Change the order of the factors and draw both arrays. Work out the total for each one.

a) 7 × 2   b) 3 × 6   c) 7 × 4   d) 5 × 8   e) 10 × 2

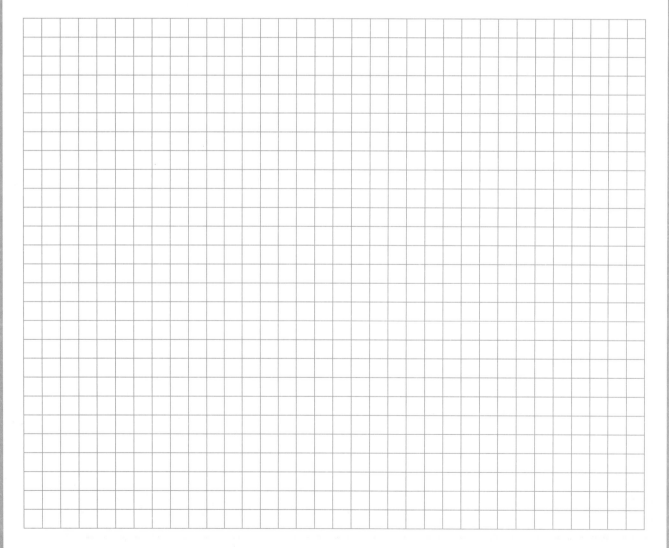

2 Match the multiplication sentence to the array.

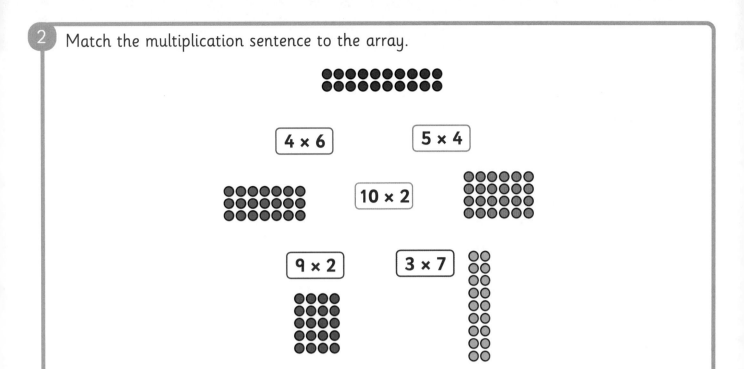

4 × 6

5 × 4

10 × 2

9 × 2

3 × 7

★ Challenge

Throw two dice. Draw a rectangle using the numbers shown on the dice as the length of its sides. For example, if you throw a 2 and a 4, you would draw a rectangle 2 boxes by 4 boxes. Write the calculation inside the rectangle you have drawn.

Can you completely fill the space below?

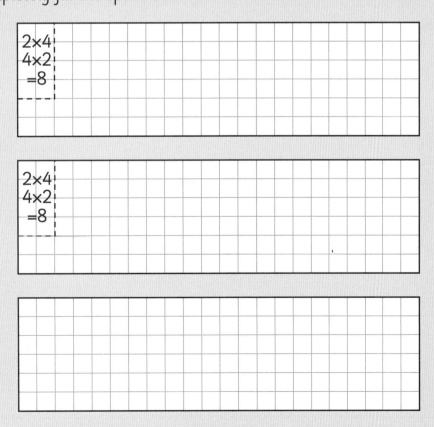

4.11 Solving multiplication problems

We can use our knowledge of 2 times table facts to help us solve multiplication problems involving 3, 4, 6 and 8 by doubling.

1 This is an array for 2 × 7:

Use this to work out the answer to these:

a) 4 × 7 = [ ]

b) 8 × 7 = [ ]

c) 3 × 7 = [ ]

d) 6 × 7 = [ ]

e) 7 × 7 = [ ]

2 Solve these problems using known facts and doubling.

One has been done for you.

2 × 12	2 × 6 = 12	Double 12	= 24
a) 3 × 18			
b) 5 × 20			
c) 4 × 15			
d) 6 × 7			

3 Amman is helping the librarian. He has boxes of books to sort. Work out how many books are in each box using facts you know and doubling.

a) two boxes of eighteen books

b) three boxes of twenty books

c) five boxes of twelve books

d) eight boxes of nine books

★ Challenge

A different way of multiplying by 8 is to double the start number and then find 4 lots of the double.

For example start with 6: 6 doubled = 12. Four lots of 12 = 48. This is the same as 6 × 8 = 48.

Another way to do this is:

6 doubled = 12   12 doubled = 24   24 doubled = 48

Use the hundred square below to track the multiples of the 2 times table and what the doubles for these are. Use a different colour for what will be the eight times table answers.

1	2	3	4	5	6	7	8	9	10
11	12	13	14	15	16	17	18	19	20
21	22	23	24	25	26	27	28	29	30
31	32	33	34	35	36	37	38	39	40
41	42	43	44	45	46	47	48	49	50
51	52	53	54	55	56	57	58	59	60
61	62	63	64	65	66	67	68	69	70
71	72	73	74	75	76	77	78	79	80
81	82	83	84	85	86	87	88	89	90
91	92	93	94	95	96	97	98	99	100

4.12 Using known facts and halving to solve division problems

We can use our knowledge of multiplication facts and halving to work out some division problems. For example, to divide by 8, half, half and then half again.

1 Use these double facts to work out the missing answers.

One has been done for you.

a) 2 × 16 = 32   32 ÷ 2 = 16   32 ÷ 4 = 8

b) 2 × 28 = 56   56 ÷ 2 = _____   56 ÷ 4 = _____

c) 2 × 32 = 64   _____ ÷ 2 = _____   _____ ÷ 4 = _____

d) 2 × 24 = _____   _____ ÷ _____ = _____   _____ ÷ _____ = _____

2 Nuria is planting seeds in window boxes.

a) She has 64 seeds and she needs to plant four seeds in each row. How many rows does she plant?

b) If she only had space for eight rows, how many seeds would need to fit in each row?

c) What would happen to your answer if she could fit 16 seeds in each row?

3 Use your knowledge of multiplication facts and halving to work out the answers to these problems:

a) 48 ÷ 4 = [   ] b) 48 ÷ 8 = [   ] c) 56 ÷ 4 = [   ]

d) 64 ÷ 8 = [   ] e) 72 ÷ 4 = [   ] f) 72 ÷ 8 = [   ]

★ Challenge

Finlay and Amman are playing a game of 'Guess my Number' together.

Finlay

If you take my number and double it, then double it again, then double it again, you get 48.

Amman

If you take my number and double it four times, you get 128.

1. What number did they begin with?

[   ]

2. Write your own 'Guess my Number' Challenge for a partner to solve.

[   ]

5.1 Recognising multiples and factors

Knowing about factors and multiples can help us solve multiplication and division problems.

1 Identify the missing factors for these number sentences.

a) _____ × 2 = 8   b) 4 × _____ = 24   c) _____ × 10 = 20

d) 5 × _____ = 40   e) _____ × 4 = 16   f) 6 × _____ = 18

2 Now identify any different factors for the multiples above.

a) _____ × _____ = 8   b) _____ × _____ = 24   c) _____ × _____ = 20

d) _____ × _____ = 40   e) _____ × _____ = 16   f) _____ × _____ = 18

3 Are these statements true or false? Circle the correct statement. If false, correct them so they make sense.

a) 12 is a multiple of 4.   True   False   _____

b) 12 is a factor of 4.   True   False   _____

c) 5 is a factor of 16.   True   False   _____

d) 25 is a multiple of 5.   True   False   _____

e) 2 and 4 are both factors of 6.   True   False   _____

f) The first three multiples of 6 are 12, 18 and 24.   True   False   _____

1. Sort these numbers into the Venn Diagram. Write them in the correct section.

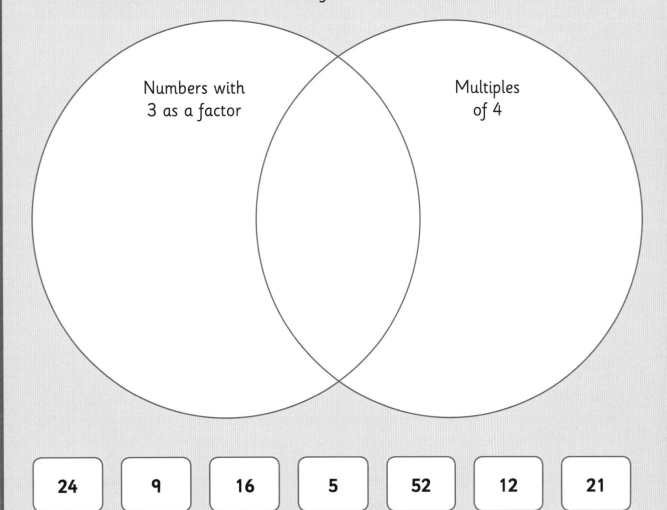

Numbers with
3 as a factor

Multiples
of 4

| 24 | 9 | 16 | 5 | 52 | 12 | 21 |

2. What other numbers would fit on the Venn Diagram?